BENJAMIN FRANKLIN
(1706–1790)

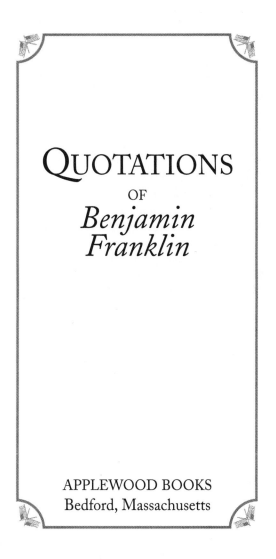

QUOTATIONS

OF
Benjamin Franklin

APPLEWOOD BOOKS
Bedford, Massachusetts

Benjamin Franklin

BENJAMIN FRANKLIN was born in Boston on January 17, 1706. As a young man, Franklin was apprenticed to an older brother, James, who published a newspaper. There, Franklin learned to set type. He read whatever books he could get his hands on and began to write. His brother was a cruel master. In 1723, at the age of seventeen, Franklin slipped away by ship to New York, where he found no work, so he went to Philadelphia.

In Philadelphia, Franklin found work as an apprentice printer. The following year, he traveled to London to purchase printing equipment to bring back to America, but his backer reneged, and Franklin stayed in England to continue his training. In 1726, Franklin returned to Philadelphia to work in a print shop. He then started his own printing business, working diligently. Soon his business thrived. In addition, he became engaged in a number of civic-minded organizations.

In 1730, Frankin married his childhood sweetheart, Deborah Read. Franklin continued to work hard, starting the *Poor Richard's Almanack* in 1733. He also continued his civic contributions, helping to found the Library Company in 1731, Philadelphia's Union Fire Company in 1736, the American Philosophical Society in

1743, the Pennsylvania Hospital in 1751, and the Philadelphia Contributionship in 1752. Many of these still exist today.

At the age of forty-two, Franklin was able to retire from business. He turned to the study of electricity. Also, he became actively interested in politics. In 1757, he went to England to represent Pennsylvania. There he stayed until 1775, as a Colonial representative not only of Pennsylvania, but of Georgia, New Jersey, and Massachusetts as well.

In 1775, after leaking British letters calling for the containment of Colonial rights, Franklin had no choice but to leave England. He came back to the Colonies where he began actively working for independence. He was elected to the Second Continental Congress and helped draft the Declaration of Independence. In 1776, Franklin signed the Declaration, and went to France as an ambassador.

During the Revolutionary War, partly because of Franklin's popularity in France, the French signed the Treaty of Alliance. Franklin was on hand to sign the Treaty of Paris in 1783, after the Revolution had been won.

In his seventies, Franklin returned to America. He became a delegate to the Constitutional Convention and signed the Constitution. Franklin died on April 17, 1790 at the age of 84.

QUOTATIONS
OF
Benjamin Franklin

$\mathcal{A}$ cheerful face is nearly as good for an invalid as healthy weather.

$\mathcal{G}$enius without education is like silver in the mine.

$\mathcal{W}$hen you're finished changing, you're finished.

$\mathcal{T}$he doors of wisdom are never shut.

*A*n undutiful daughter will prove an unmanageable wife.

*E*arly to bed and early to rise, makes a man healthy wealthy and wise.

*B*eer is living proof that God loves us and wants us to be happy.

*H*aving been poor is no shame, but being ashamed of it is.

*I*f you would not be forgotten as soon as you are dead and rotten, either write things worth reading or do things worth writing.

*T*here was never a good war, or a bad peace.

*R*eading makes a full man, meditation a profound man, discourse a clear man.

*N*ecessity never made a good bargain.

$\mathcal{A}$ good example is the best sermon.

$\mathcal{W}$ ithout continual growth and progress, such words as improvement, achievement, and success have no meaning.

$\mathcal{B}$ eware of little expenses; a small leak will sink a great ship.

$\mathcal{T}$ here are three great friends: an old wife, an old dog, and ready money.

*P*lough deep while sluggards sleep.

*T*here are two ways of being happy: We must either diminish our wants or augment our means—either may do—the result is the same and it is for each man to decide for himself and to do that which happens to be easier.

*W*e are all born ignorant, but one must work hard to remain stupid.

*Y*ou will find the key to success under the alarm clock.

Content makes poor men rich; discontent makes rich men poor.

For want of a nail the shoe was lost; for want of a shoe the horse was lost; and for want of a horse the rider was lost; being overtaken and slain by the enemy, all for the want of care about a horseshoe nail.

A learned blockhead is a greater blockhead than an ignorant one.

Drink does not drown care, but waters it, and makes it grow faster.

He was so learned that he could name a horse in nine languages; so ignorant that he bought a cow to ride on.

The heart of a fool is in his mouth, but the mouth of a wise man is in his heart.

Life's tragedy is that we get old too soon and wise too late.

Would you live with ease, do what you should, and not what you please. Success has ruined many a man.

What signifies knowing the names, if you know not the nature of things?

To succeed, jump as quickly at opportunities as you do at conclusions.

Pride that dines on vanity, sips on contempt.

He who waits upon fortune is never sure of dinner.

*B*e at war with your vices, at peace with your neighbors, and let every new year find you a better man.

*G*ood sense is a thing all need, few have, and none think they want.

*K*eep your eyes wide open before marriage, and half-shut afterwards.

*T*hose who love deeply never grow old; they may die of old age, but they die young.

Well done is better than well said.

Remember not only to say the right thing in the right place, but far more difficult still, to leave unsaid the wrong thing at the tempting moment.

Man's tongue is soft, and bone doth lack; yet a stroke therewith may break a man's back.

Historians relate, not so much what is done, as what they would have believed.

*I*n short, the way to wealth, if you desire it, is as plain as the way to market. It depends chiefly on two words, industry and frugality; that is, waste neither time nor money, but make the best use of both.

*A*ny fool can criticize, condemn and complain—and most fools do.

*E*at to live, and not live to eat.

*H*e that lives upon hope will die fasting.

*H*e that would live in peace and at ease must not speak all he knows or all he sees.

*G*lass, china, and reputation are easily cracked, and never mended well.

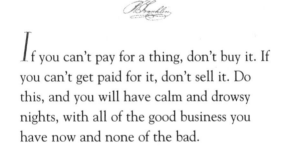

*I*f you can't pay for a thing, don't buy it. If you can't get paid for it, don't sell it. Do this, and you will have calm and drowsy nights, with all of the good business you have now and none of the bad.

*T*each your child to hold his tongue; he'll learn fast enough to speak.

*A*t 20 years of age the will reigns; at 30 the wit; at 40 the judgement.

*L*end money to an enemy, and thou will gain him, to a friend and thou will lose him.

*T*ake time for all things; great haste makes great waste.

*W*ork as if you were to live a hundred years. Pray as if you were to die tomorrow.

Were it offered to my choice, I should have no objection to a repetition of the same life from its beginning, only asking the advantages authors have in a second edition to correct some faults in the first.

Do good to your friends to keep them, to your enemies to win them.

Even peace may be purchased at too high a price.

Creditors have better memories than debtors.

*I*f a man empties his purse into his head, no man can take it away from him. An investment in knowledge always pays the best interest.

*B*e civil to all; sociable to many; familiar with few.

*G*od heals, and the doctor takes the fees.

*I*f time be of all things the most precious, wasting time must be the greatest prodigality.

*E*nergy and persistence conquer all things.

*H*e that blows the coals in quarrels that he has nothing to do with, has no right to complain if the sparks fly in his face.

*T*o lengthen thy life, lessen thy meals.

*Y*ou may delay, but time will not, and lost time is never found again.

Without justice, courage is weak.

The way to see by Faith is to shut the Eye of Reason.

Let thy child's first lesson be obedience, and the second may be what thou wilt.

If you desire many things, many things will seem few.

*B*uy what thou hast no need of, and ere long thou shalt sell thy necessaries.

*D*on't throw stones at your neighbours, if your own windows are glass.

*G*od grant that not only the love of liberty but a thorough knowledge of the rights of man may pervade all the nations of the earth, so that a philosopher may set his foot anywhere on its surface and say: "This is my country."

*H*e that cannot obey, cannot command.

*I*f you would persuade, you must appeal to interest rather than intellect.

*K*eep thy shop, and thy shop will keep thee.

*H*e that falls in love with himself will have no rivals.

*N*othing is more fatal to health than an over care of it.

The nearest way to come at glory, is to do that for conscience which we do for glory.

Wink at small faults; remember thou hast great ones.

Fear to do ill, and you need fear nought else.

How much more than is necessary do we spend in sleep, forgetting that the sleeping fox catches no poultry, and that there will be sleeping enough in the grave.

Diligence is the mother of good luck.

God helps them that help themselves.

Happiness consists more in the small conveniences of pleasures that occur every day, than in great pieces of good fortune that happen but seldom to a man in the course of his life.

Industry, perseverance, and frugality make fortune yield.

*L*earn of the skillful; he that teaches him-self, has a fool for his master.

*H*e that lies down with dogs, shall rise up with fleas.

*S*ell not virtue to purchase wealth, nor liberty to purchase power.

*T*hose disputing, contradicting, and con-futing people are generally unfortunate in their affairs. They get victory, sometimes, but they never get good will, which would be of more use to them.

Wise men don't need advice. Fools won't take it.

Many complain of their memory, few of their judgment.

They who would give up an essential liberty for temporary security, deserve neither liberty or security.

Where sense is wanting, everything is wanting.

*T*hey that won't be counseled, can't be helped.

*P*ay what you owe, and you'll know what's your own.

*I*f you would be loved, love and be lovable.

*H*e does not possess wealth that allows it to possess him.

*H*alf a truth is often a great lie.

*W*hatever is begun in anger ends in shame.

*T*he Constitution only gives people the right to pursue happiness. You have to catch it yourself.

*N*o man ever was glorious, who was not laborious.

*T*hose things that hurt, instruct.

*B*eing ignorant is not so much a shame
as being unwilling to learn.

*T*o be humble to superiors is duty, to
equals courtesy, to inferiors nobleness.

*W*e must indeed all hang together or,
most assuredly we shall all hang separately.